COULD YOU BE YOUR OWN BOSS?

Making an informed decision about starting a business – a guide for the newly-redundant

Brian O'Kane

Published by
Oak Tree Press
19 Rutland Street, Cork, Ireland
www.oaktreepress.com

A catalogue record of this book is
available from the British Library.

ISBN 978-1-904887-29-4

CONTENTS

INTRODUCTION

If you have just been made redundant, or think you might be made redundant soon, and you're thinking of starting a business, this is both a good – and a bad time – to do so.

It's a good time, because fewer people set up new businesses when the economy is doing poorly, and so you will have less competition, which means that your chance of success should be higher – remember, the Great Depression in the 1930s in the US, which followed the Wall Street Crash of 1929, created more millionaires than at any other time in American history!

On the other hand, arguably it's also a bad time – in that markets are depressed; people are not spending, because they are fearful for their own jobs; and getting investment or loans from banks is harder.

One thing is sure. Although lots of people have made lots of money starting and running their own businesses over the past 10 years, things have changed. The only businesses that will survive – let alone prosper – in the next few years will be those that truly deliver value to their customers. Let's run that sentence again: ***The only businesses that will survive – let alone prosper – in the next few years will be those that truly deliver value to their customers***.

That means you MUST plan your start-up: planning is no longer a nice-to-have, it's an absolute necessity. Otherwise, you increase your risk of failure – unnecessarily. And so, **Could You Be Your Own Boss?** does just what it says on the cover, taking you through the basics of planning a start-up, from the point where you are just thinking about it to the point where you can engage with the various enterprise support organisations in launching your new business.

The aim of this book is to help you to come to an informed decision as to whether self-employment is right for you – just now, in your present circumstances. If it is, the section **Starting Your Business** outlines what you need to do next to get started and directs you to sources of advice and training.

To turn the odds of success in your favour means that you need to understand what is likely to make your business successful. This book will help you to do just that.

Good luck.

Brian O'Kane
January 2009

PS: You'll find more information and support at our website, **www.couldyoubeyourownboss.com**.

SIGNING-UP TO SELF-EMPLOYMENT

The most critical factor in deciding whether a start-up succeeds is the entrepreneur themselves – this is you.

Your vision, your ambition, your perseverance, your willingness to work hard and long hours, your commitment, your financial resources, your skills and experience – all these are potential pluses. Against these can be set perhaps – depending on your circumstances) your inexperience in business, your lack of knowledge of the market, your personal circumstances which may restrict the time you can spend on the business, your lack of the necessary finance – all of these are potential minuses. The trick is to make sure that the pluses outweigh the minuses.

This first section of **Could You Be Your Own Boss?** looks at the nature of self-employment, so that you understand what you might be getting into, and then explores your own fit with self-employment, so that you can make an informed decision on whether it's right for you, right now. That's what this section will help you to do.

What is self-employment?

Research shows that:

o The average working week of a self-employed person is 64 hours. In almost half of all small businesses, the owner's spouse / partner is also involved for another 21 hours (together, 85 hours).

o Most people do not increase their income by becoming self-employed and 20% of entrepreneurs do not earn anything in the first 18 months.

o Almost 70% of people who decide to become self-employed do not prepare themselves properly for their new role and responsibilities.

o Specifically, almost 90% do not study their market.

o As a result, on average about 50% of all businesses in Europe fail within five years of starting.

These statistics should show you the importance of preparation and of carefully considering whether self-employment is right for you. But that's only the bad news!

There's good news too. Many entrepreneurs find immense personal satisfaction in running their own businesses, being their own boss, choosing what they do and how and when they do it – and being able to earn a living doing so. A small few make well-publicised fortunes; most get their rewards from the intangibles of self-employment.

Basically, self-employment involves:

o Doing something / anything (= opportunity).

o Getting paid for doing it (= risk).

o Being accountable for the result of your work (=responsibility).

o Planning and organising your own work (= knowledge).

o Not having a boss to tell you what to do (=
   independence).

o Finding your own work (= initiative).

o Hard work (= tough).

Being self-employed demands a lot of commitment. It is
both physically and mentally demanding. Therefore, it is
very important to ask yourself why you want to become self-
employed. It will take some soul-searching but answering
this question is vital to the decision to go ahead.

Does self-employment fit into YOUR future?

The questions below are not ones that you can answer in a few
minutes. Take your time – take plenty of time. Remember that
the answers to these questions are what will drive your business.

What do you want to get out of life?

Why are those things important to you?

What do you want to be doing in five years?

Why do you want to become self-employed?

Does self-employment fit with your vision of your life and your
future?   ❏ Yes ❏ No

Why?

Other aspects of self-employment

If self-employment is a serious option for you, it is then time to consider other aspects of it that will have an impact on your life.

Yourself

Being prepared to make the commitment does not necessarily mean that entrepreneurship is right for you. You need to answer these questions:

- o Will you be able to give the business the time and attention it needs?
- o Will your health stand up to long hours and hard work?
- o Will you be able to cope with the pressures and stress?

Your family situation

As you will need all the support you can get, it is important from the very beginning to involve your spouse / partner / family in the decision to start a business. Ask them (and listen carefully to their answers):

- o Will they commit to the business?
- o Are they prepared to accept that you will be working long hours, coming home tired and stressed out?

Make sure that they can give you the support you need.

Financial situation

Setting up a business has financial consequences. Even at this early stage, you have to consider whether you can cope with irregular income, reduced income and financial insecurity. How will this affect you and your family?

This is a very important issue because money, or lack of it, can have a huge impact on your relationships, your self-esteem and your stress levels. Think about your mortgage or rent payments, education for your children, social life, clothing, holidays, luxuries, etc.

Your view of these issues may be coloured by whether you see an opportunity – or whether you feel that redundancy leaves you no choice except self-employment. If you are excited about an opportunity that you have spotted, it's hard to be objective and to listen to well-meaning advice that urges you to be cautious – but, it's more sensible to tread a little carefully on a new path, even it chafes a little. On the other hand, if you feel you're being pushed into self-employment and are not comfortable with it, then it's unsurprising that you see negatives all around. In both cases, you need to identify and isolate your own feelings, so that you can consider self-employment without bias – not easy, but important to try to do. Talking out your idea for self-employment with someone who can offer you constructive criticism can help you look at it more objectively and is always a useful exercise.

Effects of self-employment on your life-style

How will being self-employed change your life?

How will self-employment change your spouse / partner's life?

How will self-employment change your family's life?

List some good things about being self-employed.

List some bad things about being self-employed.

How much do you need to live on?

A critical step in preparing for self-employment is to get a clear understanding of how much you actually need – as opposed to would like – to live on.

The panel on the next page will help you to estimate how much you are likely to spend in a year and thus, unless you have savings put aside, the minimum income that you must earn from your new business to get by. If you do this conscientiously, you may be surprised by how cheaply you can live!

Estimate your personal expenditure per year

For each of the items on the next page that apply to you, fill in an amount in one of the first three columns (per week / per month / per year). Some items will arise weekly – like food – while others will be monthly – like rent – and still others may be paid at different times, so you will have to use an annual figure – for example, holidays or school expenses.

Once you have made an entry for all the items that apply to you, then convert them into an annual equivalent – by multiplying by 52 for weekly items, and by 12 for monthly items – and transfer the figures into the fourth column to give an annualised amount.

What you have just calculated is what you need to earn over a year from your new business to get by and to pay all your bills. Divide the amount by 12 to get the income your business must pay you each per month: € _____.

	€ per week	€ per month	€ per year	€ annualised
Major items				
Rent/mortgage				
Food				
Clothing				
Car (insurance, tax, depreciation)				
Gas / water / electricity				
Telephone				
Insurance (health / home, etc.)				
Other household expenses				
School expenses				
Holidays				
Replacement of items like TV, washing machine, etc				
Loan repayments				
Savings				
Other expenses				
Total expenditure [A]				
Deductions				
Other earnings (apart from your proposed business)				
Government benefits				
Rent subsidies				
Total Deductions [B]				
Total expenditure that your business must pay for each year [A – B]				

Remember that the amount shown at the bottom of the panel is the amount that you need to earn from your business – not the amount of sales your business needs to generate. After all, the business will have to pay for stock, marketing, rent and insurance, perhaps staff and other overheads, before it can pay you anything.

And, until your business is able to pay you this amount regularly every month, this is the amount that you will have to take from your savings each month in order to live. Bear that in mind when calculating how much you can afford to invest in your new business.

Skills & Experience

Running your own business takes certain personal skills and experience. You should assess yourself to see what skills you have already and which skills you need to develop.

During your life, you pick up all kinds of skills. Some of these are the formal skills you learnt at school or work – how to speak French, how to use a wood lathe or how to use a computer spreadsheet.

But you probably also have other skills, learnt at home or in social situations – how to deal with difficult people who are always finding fault without losing your temper, how to balance a budget or how to get people to do what you want them to do when you cannot give them direct orders or instructions.

When you think for a few moments, you will be amazed at how many skills you have and how many may be transferable to business generally. For example:

- o Looking after the home and raising a family gives you skills in time-keeping, finance, administration, communication, management, etc.

- o Organising the neighbourhood barbecue gives you skills in planning, organising and motivating people, etc. Running marathons teaches you determination and self-discipline.

o Even socialising in pubs helps you communicate and budget and teaches you the importance of timing ("Last orders now, please!").

Look at your education and your experience – not just experience at work but also hobbies, community activities, your family situation, etc. Are these experiences related to your business idea? (If you don't have a business idea yet, don't worry – you can come back and answer these questions later.) Can you tap into what you have already learnt?

Now look at the areas where you might have problems:

o How good are you at selling? At book-keeping?
o Can you do price calculations quickly in your head – or do you always need a calculator?
o Can you manage people?
o Can you work with your hands?
o Can you deal with customers?

When you come to consider your business idea (if you don't have a business idea yet, don't worry – you can come back and answer these questions later), ask yourself:

o What tasks can you do yourself already?
o In which areas do you need help?
o In which areas do you need training?

You do not have to be superman or superwoman to be an entrepreneur. There is no golden formula. What you need is a good understanding of your capabilities and the willingness to fill in the gaps, either by additional training for yourself or by hiring other people to do the necessary work.

What are you good at?

Skills:
-
-
-
-

Practical experience:
-
-
-
-

Skills in family:
-
-
-
-

Practical skills in family:
-
-
-
-

Hobbies / interests:
-
-
-
-

What other skills do you think you need for your business?
-
-
-
-

What skills would you like to improve?
-
-
-
-

What training do you need?
-
-
-
-

What does success mean to you?

This another important question, which will have a major influence on the kind of business that you set up (see **Finding an Idea**) and on how happy and fulfilled – or otherwise – you will be as you progress your idea to reality and beyond.

Success is not always measured in material terms: being free to work on projects that interest you, with people you like, at times that suit you, may be more valuable than 10%, or 20%, or even 100% more income.

Only you can decide what success means to you. There's no "right" answer but is helpful to give the question some thought as you consider self-employment.

In this section of **Could You Be Your Own Boss?**, you have looked at yourself, you have looked into the effect that self-employment will have on your life and you have studied aspects of entrepreneurship.

By now, you should be fully aware what you are getting yourself into. If you have not been honest when answering the questions, it is time to think again. It is no use fooling yourself because it will catch up with you in the end.

So, are you ready for the next step?

FINDING AN IDEA

For most people – especially those who have not previously given a lot of thought to the notion of self-employment – this is the hardest thing about starting a business, deciding what kind of business it will be or what it will sell or make.

Basically, there are three ways of coming up with an idea for a business: copy, create, or find a growing sector.

Then you need to consider the type of business that you're aiming to start.

Copying ideas

Look around you. There are millions of businesses out there already – more than 200,000 in Ireland alone. Some of them may be copyable, or adaptable, or may give you an idea for a new business.

Go back to your skills and experience (see **Signing-up to Self-Employment**). Where could they be used? In particular, where could they be used to save other people money – since that's the one thing that everyone becomes very conscious of in a downturn. For example, people who previously would have thought nothing of buying a new pair of shoes when the ones they had began to show a little bit of wear will now be seeking out a cobbler or shoe-repairer to extend the life of the shoes and to put off the time when they must be replaced. Can you think of other ways in which people could save money – and you could help them do so?

Alternatively, look at bigger businesses – which often miss out on the personal element that is so important for good customer / business relationships – and see whether you could start a similar business, on a smaller scale perhaps, but with that human touch?

Could you outsource work that you used to do from the business where you used to work? If you have not already been made redundant, this could form part of your exit negotiations.

Have you seen something on holidays – a product, or service, or business – that you could not find at home? Perhaps you could adapt this idea for Irish customers?

The most obvious way of copying a good idea is by franchising it. Lots of businesses – especially service businesses – grow by franchising their business idea, and the underlying systems and brand, to other people.

Creating ideas

This where the true entrepreneur comes in – they see opportunities where no one else can.

Developing your idea to its fullest potential involves creative thinking. The creative thinking techniques below will help you to identify new ideas, develop your existing idea and create new opportunities.

Technique 1: Brainstorming

1. Get a group together (Four people is the minimum, preferably more).
2. Define a problem and then redefine it.
3. Then brainstorm:
   > Aim to generate as many ideas as possible.
   > All ideas are acceptable.
   > The crazier the idea, the better.
4. Select the craziest idea and brainstorm that idea.

For example, see how many uses you can find for a paperclip.

Technique 2: Attribute listing

This technique is usually used when you are thinking of adapting or developing an existing product or service but it can be used to create a new product or service from an existing one.

Take the particular product / service and list its attributes: For example, shape, size, design, materials, colour, functions and cost. Then take each attribute and try to find as many alternatives to it as possible.

Technique 3: Who, what, where, when, why, how

Tease out different perspectives and ideas with any product, service, problem or situation, using the six prompts above. For example, who buys product X now? If we wanted to make product X appeal to an entirely different group of customers, how would we have to change the product, its price and the way we market it to be sure that they would buy it?

Technique 4: Assumption-smashing

List the assumptions of the problem or idea, then explore what happens if you drop assumptions. For example, why assume that this booklet should be available only in printed form. What if it were available as an MP3 download? How would that change the market for it?

Technique 5: Discontinuity

Disrupt your own patterns:

- o Programme interruptions in your day.
- o Do something you have never done before or read something you would not normally read.
- o Watch some different TV programmes.

Be careful, though – it's easy to be creative and to come up with clever ideas for possible businesses. Once the creative burst is over, look at your ideas again in the cold light of day and see whether they really stack up. That's where your market research (see **Evaluating Your Idea**) comes into its own.

Find a growing sector

This is more general advice perhaps than specific guidance on finding a business idea – but it's useful nonetheless.

If you can identify a sector that still thrives, even in a downturn, and can find a place for yourself in that sector, then not only will you create a business for now but you should be creating one that will flourish when the good times return. Examples of these kinds of sector include: green / environmental, education and IT.

There's no doubt that some green initiatives will be undertaken in the next few years because they save people or the Government money, but there's a clear trend towards a greater awareness of things environmental – just ask your children, you'll be amazed at how much more clued in they are than your own generation. Can you find somewhere within this trend where your skills and experience can be put to good use?

Or in education? In a knowledge economy, which is what we have today, this is essential, not just for children but for everyone. Lifelong learning is / was a buzzword – but it's a genuine and lasting trend too – and one that offers lots of opportunities, if only you can find the right one for yourself.

And IT is the same. Yes, at one level, it's the preserve of geeks, with their strange jargon and incomprehensible computer terms. But everyone uses computers, for almost everything, these days. If you can explain their use, manage them, keep them running, fix them, whatever, is there an opportunity there for you?

Start, buy or franchise?

In most cases, people considering self-employment think first about starting their own business – but there are alternatives.

Buying an existing business

Buying an existing business can be a sensible alternative to starting a business from scratch. The main advantage is that the business has existing products, markets, customers, staff, etc. and you don't have to build them all up yourself. The disadvantage is that, usually, a considerable investment is needed to acquire the business, and more money may have to be added to develop it further.

And, just like when buying a second-hand car, it is also important to know why the business is being sold – perhaps the business is in trouble or is about to face major competition, which might depress profits in the future. This investigation is called "due diligence" and involves you (or an accountant or consultant on your behalf) examining:

o   Financial data – what do the figures show?

o   Management and key staff – how to retain them?

o   Recent investments (or lack of).

o   Product development / improvements (or lack of).

o   Innovation (or lack of).

o   Use of modern technology (or lack of).

o   Hidden liabilities.

The key issue is the value of the business – what you will have to pay for it – which is determined by its potential for earning profit in the future. Remember that previous years' profits are a guide to future earnings but cannot always be relied on, especially in a downturn.

You should always take professional advice when buying a business, to make sure that what you are buying is as described and that you have protected yourself against the risk of future liabilities. You don't want to pay a lot of money for a business, only then to find out that it owes a lot of money to people the previous owner didn't tell you about – money that you will probably have to stump up.

Use the checklist below to guide your purchase of an existing business.

Buying into a business

1. Why is the business for sale?

2. What is the business of the company?

3. How is it organised?

4. What is its position in the market-place?

5. What are its future prospects?

6. Is there a current Business Plan? What does it tell me?

7. Does the culture of the company fit my style of working and managing?

8. How dependent is the company on the current owner / managers?

Where will you find a business to buy? From time to time, you may find them in the classified sections of the newspapers. Talk to your local accountant, who may have clients who want to dispose of a business. And then there are business brokers, who act as agents for people who want to sell businesses, just like estate agents do for houses and offices. (See the Business Sales / Purchases category in the   Assistance   section   of **www.startingabusinessinireland.com** for a range of known sources.)

Usually, it's more expensive to buy a business than to start a similar business from scratch. Against this, you have to weigh the fact that you can start straight away with a decent level of turnover, with existing customer and supplier bases, all systems in place, etc, rather than taking several years to get to that stage.

Buying into a franchise
Across the world, there are over 3,000 franchised businesses, covering almost every industry. Some are international brands like McDonald's; others are national brands like O'Brien's Sandwich Bars; a few are much smaller, local opportunities.

When you buy a franchise, you buy the right to use a specific trademark or business concept, which has been tested in practice. The chief benefit is that you are able to capitalise on the business format, trade name, and support system provided by the franchisor.

In return for an initial upfront fee and ongoing fees for the right to the franchise, the franchisor supplies a detailed operational manual, which sets out exactly how to run the franchise. It is also usual for franchisees to pay into a co-operative national advertising and promotional fund, which benefits all franchises through increased exposure to the common trade name.

The advantages of buying a franchise are:

o A much lower failure rate than other start-up businesses, since most of the problems have been discovered and solved.

o A complete package, including trademarks, easy access to an established product, proven marketing method, equipment, stock, financial and accounting systems, on-going training and support, research and development, sales and marketing assistance, planning and forecasting, etc.

However, the essence of a franchise – buying and operating a proven concept – can make it seem like you are more of a manager than a boss, since the franchise agreement is a binding contract, and sometimes can be quite restrictive.

Franchises are not for everyone – but they do offer an alternative entry route to self-employment, with a lower risk threshold. Since the business concept has already been tested by other franchisees, there's less risk of failure – typically, franchises have a 70%+ start-up success rate, compared to the normal 50% start-up rate. Banks usually are happier lending to a franchise start-up because of the lower risk.

Use the checklist on the next page to guide your purchase of a franchise.

Buying into a franchise

1. Does the franchisor have a record of success?   o YES o NO

2. What will it cost me?   My current income? o
                                       Twice my current income? o
                                                      More? o

3. How much can I expect to make?   My current income? o
                                  Twice my current income? o
                                                 More? o

4. Will the franchisor give me an exclusive territory for the
   period of the franchise?   o YES o NO

5. Will the franchisor assist me with:
   a) A management training programme?   o YES o NO
   b) An employee training programme?   o YES o NO
   c) A PR and advertising programme?   o YES o NO
   d) Raising capital   o YES o NO
   e) Borrowing money?   o YES o NO
   f)   Merchandising ideas?   o YES o NO
   g) Finding a suitable location?   o YES o NO

6. How long has the franchisor been operating?
                                  Less than 3 years? o
                                  More than 3 years? o

7. Has the franchisor a reputation for fair dealing with its
   franchisees?   o YES o NO

8. Has the franchisor enough finance itself to carry out its plans?
                                                 o YES o NO

9. What happens when I want to leave / give up?
   Can I sell the business to anyone I like?   o YES o NO

10. Has the franchisor shown me any certified figures indicating
    exact net profits of one or more franchisees, which I have
    personally checked with them?   o YES o NO

11. Has the franchisor investigated me enough to be sure that
     I can operate at a profit to both of us?   o YES o NO

12. Is my lawyer happy with the franchise contract? o YES o NO

Adapted from *Making Money* magazine by permission.

Starting a new business from scratch

This is the conventional path to self-employment – it's what this booklet is mainly about. It means coming up with the idea, planning it, financing it, and then executing it. In most cases, you will be forced far beyond your comfort zone, into areas that you know nothing about. And, because of that, it's risky – if you don't know what you are doing, the risks of making a mistake, especially a fatal mistake, are greater. International studies repeatedly show that, typically, 50% of start-ups fail within the first few years.

But it's not all doom and gloom either! Thousands of people start new businesses every day – and about half of them survive and succeed! Those who do usually attribute their success to planning. So don't dismiss starting from scratch – but don't underestimate the challenges it poses either!

The *Global Entrepreneurship Monitor Report for Ireland 2007* suggests that 1 in 12 Irish people were involved in actively planning or had recently started a business; among 25-34 year-olds, this figure increased to 1 in 9. So you're not alone!

Your next step, which is still part of finding a business idea, is to decide what kind of business you want to start. Some businesses sell time, others sell product, while a very few disrupt whole industries – which is yours? Your business could be a "lifestyle" or a "growth" business; it could be local, national or global; it could be product or service-based; it could buy-in product or manufacture in-house – only you can decide. Read on ...

Sell time, sell product or disrupt?

Effectively, lots of small businesses do no more than sell their owner's time and skill – for example, a plumber sells his / her time, even if they don't charge by the hour, because when they are not working, they don't get paid. Accountants, consultants, tradespeople, anyone with a saleable skill, does the same. This kind of business is easy to get into – provided that you have the necessary skill and experience in an area that people are willing to pay for – but its growth is limited to the number of hours' work that you, or your staff, can deliver.

Moving to a situation where you sell a "product" usually involves greater financial commitment and a bigger, better-resourced organisation, since the product has to be made before it can be sold. So you need raw materials, manufacturing processes, factories and warehouses, etc – or you buy in finished products in bulk from someone else who makes them. Either way, there's more outlay and risk – but potentially better reward.

The really enormous rewards come in businesses based on "disruptive technologies", ones that completely change the way that people do things in a particular area. For example, look at the impact that fax, email and mobile phones have had on communications: when post and landline phones were the only ways of communicating with people, communications were slow and / or expensive over long distances and people had difficulty changing arrangements at short notice; now, email removes distance as a barrier, while Skype / VOIP phones remove cost as a barrier, while mobile phones remove the need to be at a specific location in order to receive and take calls. And, fewer and fewer people post letters, except where some kind of physical document needs to be sent – for example, a contract or a birthday card. Fax, email and mobile phones have disrupted the conventional ways of doing things. The risk and rewards here are much, much higher – for every one successful disruptive technology, there are thousands that fail. And it's not always the pioneers who reap the rewards – usually, it's the people who come behind them, who avoid the mistakes and enter the market after it has been educated to understand, to use and to value the new technology.

"Life-style" or "growth"?

There are lots of different types of business, but the two extremes are "life-style" businesses and "growth" businesses. Of course, there are lots of other types in between, though they lack descriptive names.

A "life-style" business is one where the owner usually makes a good living from the business, without working too hard, or working the long and unsocial hours often associated with self-employment. It's one where the owner makes a conscious choice of putting their own life-style before business success – and usually sacrifices some, or most, of the potential of the business in the process. Think of a beach-side bar in the tropics, where the owner rises late, surfs through until mid-afternoon and, after a lengthy siesta, opens for business for a few hours in the evening, closes when he feels like it and not according to a printed schedule – that's a life-style business! Another example is the consultant who moves from a high-flying director-level job to a rural location, in order to spend more time with his / her family, earning a basic living from perhaps more mundane work locally.

In contrast, some businesses – a small minority – are "growth" businesses, which have both the potential for real and rapid expansion and an owner who is prepared to make the necessary sacrifices to achieve that potential. It's the last bit that's important – and where the contrast with life-style businesses is most apparent: in what the owner is prepared to sacrifice, and for what.

Neither one nor the other type of business is "better" – although from the point of view of the economy and of the enterprise support bodies, a growth business is preferred as a better investment for support. But again, it's your business, and you need to choose what suits you. You need to go back to the start of this book and look at your answers and judge the suitability of a business type against them, rather than against someone else's notion.

Local, national or international?

Most service businesses are local, since it's hard to ensure that a service is delivered the right way, every time, if you are not there on the spot yourself, either to do it yourself or to make sure that it is done right by your staff. And, if it can be done the right way with no supervision, then it's likely that the business can be easily copied – think of sandwich or coffee shops.

Often, Irish businesses need to aim at being national, in order to find enough customers. But this requires resources – both in marketing to, and serving, customers across a wider territory. For service businesses, the challenge is to systematise what they do, to ensure the same standards of delivery in all locations.

There are only about five million people in Ireland altogether – about the same as a decent-sized international city! And, for this reason, ambitious Irish businesses have to export very early in their development – simply to find enough customers, the Irish market is just not big enough for them. However, exporting is even more difficult than selling locally, since there's often language, and always cultural and regulatory, barriers to be overcome. Although you should not underestimate the challenge involved in growing an international business, you also should know that the enterprise support bodies are especially keen on supporting this kind of business – or one that can show that it has international potential.

Product-based or service-based?

Every business sells some kind of product or service – sometimes one or the other, sometimes a mixture of both – to its customers.

Product-based businesses usually involve:

o An investment in stock – of raw materials or parts for manufacture or assembly of the product, or of finished items ready for re-sale.

o A distribution channel to customers.

o A physical location that suits customers.

These things all cost money. Stock clearly costs money, since you have to pay for it – often before you can sell it, which puts pressure on your cash flow. But there's also the risk of making or buying the wrong stock – wrong size, wrong colours, wrong model – or of obsolescence, where your stock goes out-of-date – food past its sell-by date, for example, or "old" technology, even though it works perfectly well.

The choice of distribution channel to reach customers is often a manufacturer's greatest challenge. Every distribution channel involves costs – whether you sell direct to the end-customer, bearing all the marketing costs yourself, or you sell through intermediaries, such as wholesalers and retailers, who are rewarded by commissions or discounts from the retail price.

And it is rare for any manufacturer to have just one channel of distribution – most have, and need, several, in order to reach into different parts of the market. For example, Dell, which has been so successful in selling direct to customers is now partnering with major US retailers, like Best Buy, Staples, Wal-Mart and Sam's Club, to offer pre-configured, pre-built computers – just like the other computer manufacturers that have always sold through the retail channel. But Dell is not turning its back on what has made it successful – it is simply recognising that, while a large part of the market wants to customise computers to their own specifications and will buy and wait a few days for delivery to do so, a significant part of the computer user market will do neither of these things – they want to walk into a store, buy a reliable computer, with a sensible specification, from a recognisable brand, and to walk out the door with it, take it home, plug it in and start using it immediately. They are prepared to trade off customisability for immediate usability (again, this shows the importance of understanding what customers are really buying).

And last, physical location. This can be critical for many businesses, especially those in retail or personal services, or those that need specific resources close at hand – deep-sea ports, rivers, access to raw materials, suppliers, or skilled staff. A restaurant located on an unfashionable street or unfashionable part of town will be less successful than one in a better (from the customers' point of view) location. But physical location can be irrelevant for businesses that sell at a distance from their customers – mail order or Internet-based businesses, for example – or consultants, who travel to their clients' businesses to carry out their work.

Service-based businesses sell "intangibles" like haircuts, or accounting services. Very often, potential customers cannot tell whether the service is good or bad until after they have bought it – and sometimes not even then, if they lack the necessary expertise to judge the quality of the service. This makes it harder for customers to compare – and so they are often slow to try a new supplier of a service (because of the risk of making a bad choice), and (good news, perhaps) even slower to change once they feel that they are getting a good deal. So, in selling services, you need to think to think about how you can reduce the risk to a potential customer of that first, all important, trial.

Service businesses are "people" businesses – they depend on their staff to deliver the service, whether it is a haircut, accounting services, a meal, or a car service. And the challenge of a service business is consistency of service delivery. If you go to the same hairdresser or restaurant, you won't receive exactly the same service every time – if the restaurant is very busy, short-staffed, with problems in the kitchen and the manager away on holiday, you'll get a less than wonderful experience.

Systematising service delivery is an essential first step if you have ambitions to develop your service business through franchising – if you can't show someone else how to run your business, you can't franchise it – but it's also important for keeping customers. Reducing the variability of service delivery is a key way to get customers coming back again and again – that favourite restaurant of yours is your favourite in large part because of its consistency, it rarely disappoints.

Evaluating Your Idea

The previous section helped you to find your idea. Finding a good idea is important since it is the second most critical factor in deciding whether a start-up succeeds. It's not so much the idea itself – lots of arguably poor ideas do exceptionally well, while excellent ideas fall by the wayside – but what matters is the match between your idea and the needs of the marketplace.

The key questions here are:

o Will anybody want to buy my product / service?

o Who?

o Why? (and Why from me?)

o When? (and How often?)

o Where?

The first question is the most important – and it is the one that is most often skipped over by would-be entrepreneurs in their rush to get to market. That way lies failure – sometimes fast, sometimes, slow, but always certain.

The only way that you can answer the question of whether anybody will want to buy your product or service is by asking people, by doing market research.

You need to be very objective and hard-nosed about your market research. Don't assume – check things out yourself. Don't accept what people tell you – again, check it out. Don't let your passion for your product / service and your enthusiasm blind you to the reality of the marketplace – that perhaps your product / service is not wanted, or not wanted in that shape / size / format, or at that price, or in that location – whatever. And the only way you will find out is by asking people – potential customers.

Market research

Market statistics

In an ideal world, the first step in market research is to put together some statistics on the market that you are aiming for – for example:

- o How big is it?
- o Where is it?
- o Is it growing or contracting?

However, unless you have a very large, high-level definition market in mind, it will be hard to get those statistics, since usually officially-published statistics are aggregated. So, for example, if you're looking for market statistics on "electrical products", you'll probably find what you are looking for – at least on a national level. But, if you're looking to know how many iPods were sold in Carlow in the first six months of 2008 – good luck!

However, that said, there are probably less than a dozen shops in Carlow that sell iPods, so you could go around all of them, armed with a clipboard and a questionnaire, and ask the manager of each shop how many they sold in the period. Even if they don't give you an exact number – most will be concerned about competition and confidentiality – they may give you a range ("more than 10 and less than 100"), which is better than nothing.

The Central Statistics Office has a useful, and little-known, product called SAPS – Small Area Population Statistics – which will give you demographic information, right down to the level of townlands. So, while it won't tell you how many iPods were sold in Carlow in a particular time-period, SAPS will tell you how many people in different age groups live in Carlow – town or county – and some background on them.

Check with your local library – or the main library in your nearest town – and with your County or City Enterprise Board or other enterprise support organisation locally – they may have done some research in the area, or be aware of research done locally, that may be useful in filling in some of the picture for you.

Identifying your customer

You should have some intuitive idea of the customers your business is going to target. Use your market research to confirm this.

Can you write a profile of your typical customer? Can you distinguish your customers from those of your competitors? How can you identify your customers from among the many people in the town, city or country in which you are located? This is critical because, unless you can identify your customers, how will you know how to reach them?

What are the defining characteristics of your customers:

o Are they old or young?

o Are they rich or poor?

o Do they have children? Babies or teenagers?

o Where do they live?

o What kinds of cars do they drive?

o Do they take foreign holidays? How often? And where?

o Do they use the Internet?

o Have they credit cards? Which ones? How much do they use them? And for what?

o Do they buy locally or will they buy by post or over the telephone?

o Do they respond to television advertising?

There are hundreds of questions that you can ask about your customers that will help you to define who they are. Without this customer profile firmly in your mind, most of your marketing effort will be no more than random shots into the dark.

Understanding consumer behaviour

Then you need to understand their behaviour. Start by finding out what elements in your service or product are most important to your customers. To understand fully your customers' needs, make sure to clarify exactly what the customer means by probing until you are clear what the real needs are. For example, if customers say they want "Total quality", ask "What do you mean by that?". When they answer "Quick response", you ask "What do you mean by quick response?". After asking "What do you mean?" a few times, you will establish the real need.

You also need to understand when and where your potential customers expect to buy. These two may be linked: for example, if this is a once-off purchase with little maintenance required, it's likely that the customer will shop around for the cheapest price, even it if means buying from further away or over the internet.; whereas, if the product requires ongoing support, they may consider it worthwhile to pay a little more to have local support available. This is why people are happy to buy furniture in IKEA in Belfast, while, if they are not technically-minded, they will buy a computer for home or business use from a local supplier, even if the supplier is more expensive.

Competitors

Your market research should also help you to identify your competitors.

Your competition can come in different forms. It can be local, national or, increasingly, international. It can be direct (someone who provides the same, or very similar, product or service) or indirect (someone who provides something completely different, but which takes potential spending power from your customer).

Ask yourself these questions to identify and assess your competitors:

o What are the alternatives for your products or services?

o Who makes / sells these alternatives?

o What range of products or services do they have?

o What kind of choices do they offer customers?

o How broad is their range?

o What are their target groups?

o What are their future prospects?

o What are they good at and what are they not so good at?

The key to winning at competition – especially indirect competition – is to understand your customers and why they buy (or don't buy) from you.

Note that market research should be an ongoing process. It should not stop after the business has started but should become an integral part of your business.

Practical market research

Practical market research includes things as simple as:

Counting the cars on your competitors' parking lot (to tell you how many customers they get and how well-off they are).

Counting the people passing by the premises you are planning to rent (big stores like Marks & Spencer sometimes do this for months before deciding on a location for a new shop).

Counting the waste bags outside the backdoor of a restaurant (to give you some idea of the volume of their business).

Checking the number of trucks delivering supplies to competitors (on the basis that level of their purchases gives you an insight into their sales).

Counting the numbers of customers walking into a competitor's office / shop.

Knocking on every door in a housing estate in which you are planning to open an outlet (to ask whether there is a demand, at what price, etc.).

Collecting all your competitors' brochures and price lists (to find out what they are offering and at what prices).

Checking where your competitors advertise and how big an advertisement they take.

FINDING MONEY & HELP

Two of the greatest challenges that most start-up entrepreneurs face are finding enough money to get started and finding help in researching and planning their business.

Often, for those who have been made redundant recently, the first is not a problem. Your redundancy package may have given you a significant lump sum – often, more money than you have ever seen in one place at a time! The hard part in this situation is not finding the money – you have it already – but hanging on to it and using it wisely. It's tempting to rush into spending when money is available – so be sensible.

But, despite a redundancy package, you still may not have enough money to get started in your chosen business – or, sensibly, you may have decided to limit your start-up risk by putting some of your redundancy out of reach. So you need additional funding.

The other challenge, common to all entrepreneurs, is finding help in getting started. That help might be practical – market research information, training, mentoring – or moral – encouragement, support, understanding. Either way, you need to know what you need and know where to look for it.

This section will help you to locate both funding and assistance.

Types of finance

There are basically only two types of finance:

o **Equity** – Capital invested in the business, usually not repayable until the business closes down finally.

o **Debt** – Capital lent to the business, usually repayable at a specified date.

There are also only two sources:

o Your own money.

o Someone else's money.

Owners' Equity

If you are putting equity into the business (and you MUST – if you won't, who else will!), recognise that this investment will be at risk. Decide whether there are assets you want to keep in your personal name or which you are not prepared to put up as security or to mortgage. Identify these and then look at everything else you own:

o How easily could they be sold and what would they fetch?

o Are they mortgagable assets?

o Will they be acceptable as collateral?

Before you mortgage your family home, obtain professional advice. Consider:

o Ownership of the property.

o The impact of the Family Home Protection Act.

o What would happen to the family home and your family if the business fails.

o The approach that the banks and the courts take in such circumstances.

It is important that you raise as much as you can from your own resources, since most financiers work on a "matching funds" basis – they will invest no more than you are investing. This may mean being creative and including as part of your investment some items that would have been available to the business on an informal basis anyway. For example, if you plan to start a software business, you probably have your own PC and peripherals and probably intended using these in the business until it could afford to buy newer (and faster) machines. Put a value on them and include them as part of your investment, which might now be made up of €3,000 cash and €10,000 equipment – which looks better than just €3,000 cash!

If you can raise all the money you need from your own resources, then you can count yourself lucky and move further on in this section. Everyone else, keep reading!

External Equity

Before you raise external equity, you need to be prepared to allow other people to own part of your business. Sounds logical, but many entrepreneurs forget this and react badly when their investors begin to want some involvement in the business in return for their investment.

If you are looking for external equity, there are three types to consider:

o **Seed capital** – Less than €125,000, for start-ups.

o **Venture capital** – Between €125,000 and €600,000, for businesses at an early stage of development.

o **Development capital** – €600,000+, for companies ready to expand.

Seed capital is the one you probably want. Unfortunately, it is also the hardest to get, although the recent success of Irish technology companies means that there's plenty of funding available, sometimes linked to incubation facilities.

Nonetheless, external equity is usually only available to businesses that can demonstrate clear growth plans that will deliver an above average financial return to the investor – it's not for everyone.

See the Equity category in the Assistance section of **www.startingabusinessinireland.com** for a range of known sources of external equity.

Owners' Debt

This is not a major source of finance for start-ups, since other investors prefer to see the owners' investment in the form of equity (more permanent than loans). However, it may be appropriate to put some part of your investment in the business as a loan (and thus repayable). Take your accountant's advice here.

External Debt

Debt comes in a variety of forms, from a simple loan from a friend with few conditions attached, through overdrafts, term loans, long-term loans, mortgages, etc. Debt finance available to start-ups includes:

- o **Overdraft** – The simplest form of bank finance. Basically, this is no more than permission to have a minus balance on your bank account. However, overdrafts must be cleared (and stay cleared for at least 30 days during the year, though not necessarily consecutive days) on an annual basis and the overdraft is repayable on demand.

- o **Term loan** – A loan for a fixed period, usually at a variable rate. Repayments include interest and capital.

- o **Long-term loans** – Often subsidised by Government or EU schemes, these aim to provide businesses with capital for 7 to 10 years.

- o **Mortgages** – Loans to buy business property, secured on the property itself, with fixed or variable rate options.

- o **Leasing** – A way of acquiring the use of fixed assets (for example, plant and machinery, cars, office equipment) by paying a regular monthly or quarterly payment, which is usually allowable for tax purposes. At the end of the lease, depending on the terms, you may have the option to continue using the asset for a small continuing payment or to buy it outright from the lessor.

- o **Invoice discounting** – A facility linked directly to sales, which maximises the cash value of current assets. The bank will pay you, say, 80% of the face value of an invoice when it is issued. The balance, less charges, will be paid to you when the invoice is paid. Useful for the company that is expanding and in danger of being choked for lack of cash.

When considering financing your business with debt, you must consider:

- o Fixed or floating.
- o Long-term or short-term.

Fixed debt is a loan that is secured on a specific asset – for example, on premises. Floating debt is secured on assets that change regularly – for example, debtors.

"Secured" means that, in the event that the loan is not repaid, the lender can appoint a "receiver" to sell the asset on which the loan is secured in order to recover the amount due. Thus, giving security for a loan is not something to be done lightly.

Because you have to pay interest on debt, you should try to manage with as little as possible. However, few businesses get off the ground without putting some form of debt on the balance sheet. The issues are usually:

o What is the cheapest form of debt available?

o What is the right balance between debt and equity?

o How to reduce the amount of borrowing required?

o Will borrowing be backed by personal assets?

It is a good idea to try to match the term of the loan to the type of asset that you are acquiring:

o To avoid constant renewing / restructuring problems.

o To ensure that each loan is covered by the break-up value of the assets in case of disaster.

For example, a loan to buy premises should be a long-term loan, unless you can see clearly that you will have enough money within a short space of time to repay it. Taking out a short-term loan or overdraft to buy premises is a recipe for disaster. You will have to renegotiate it time and again – and, if your business runs into temporary difficulties, you run the risk of losing everything if the bank calls in the loan.

Short-term loans, or even overdrafts, are more suited to funding stock or debtors because you should be able to repay the loan once you have sold the goods or got the money in. Short-term finance is also used to fund other forms of working capital and cash flow. It should always be repaid within the year – even if at the end of the period you still need to borrow more to fund future cash flow. If you have to borrow the same sum of money against the same asset for longer than a year at a time, you should be considering longer-term finance.

If disaster strikes and you have to repay the loan, it will be much easier to do so if the value of the assets it was used to fund is roughly equivalent to the value of the loan. Thus, for instance, you would hope to sell your premises for at least as much as you borrowed to buy them. Machinery may be more difficult, as the resale price is rarely comparable with the purchase price. For this reason, unless the equipment you need is very specialised, consider buying second-hand for your start-up.

If you can, you should arrange your loans so that unrealisable (or slow to realise) assets are purchased out of your own equity, using borrowing only for realisable assets. If an asset is easily realisable, the bank is much more likely to accept it as security.

See the Debt category in the Assistance section of **www.startingabusinessinireland.com** for a range of known sources of external equity.

How much money do you need?

It's hard to tell how much money you will need to start your business – at least until after you have prepared a complete business plan, including financial projections (see the next section) – but it's usually more than you think at first.

Without being unduly pessimistic (there's nothing more off-putting to an investor or banker than an entrepreneur who appears not to believe in his / her own project), you need to leave yourself a reasonable margin of security.

You might not be able to raise all the funds you think necessary but a useful calculation is to work out what it would cost you to get your business up and running and to keep it open for 12 months – without any sales or other income. Extreme, yes – but useful to know, because that's your worst case. If you can't get the business bringing in cash within 12 months, it probably won't work.

Another useful calculation is "cash burn" – calculate how many months' spending your financing represents. In other words, if you got no further investment and made no sales, how many months could you keep the business open? Clearly, the higher the figure, the better your margin of security.

Support from State agencies

There is a wide range of State bodies charged with assisting entrepreneurs and potential entrepreneurs to develop their businesses. The assistance they provide may be in the form of cash grants but increasingly includes advice, subsidies, training, workspace, etc.

Whatever form it takes, this assistance may be vital in providing the final piece of the jigsaw to get your business up and running, or it may provide just the push you need to get going. Sometimes, it may even be just the fact that someone else has confidence in you that makes it all come together.

Grant-aid, or other assistance, is a good thing. It can help your business to grow. Going through the application process, whether or not you are successful, will focus your planning. But don't let the need to meet grant-givers' criteria push your business where you don't want to go.

The structure of State support for enterprise

Overall responsibility for enterprise lies with the Department of Enterprise, Trade & Employment (DETE), which is responsible for promoting competitiveness in the economy and for creating a favourable climate for the creation of self-sustaining employment. It works to monitor and improve the environment for business by ensuring that the framework of law, regulation and Government policy promotes effective company performance and both public and business confidence.

DETE achieves this indirectly by creating an environment for enterprise and directly through the agencies it has established, which operate to stimulate industrial development at different levels:

o **Nationally** – Enterprise Ireland.

o **Regionally** – Shannon Development and Údarás na Gaeltachta.

o **Locally** – County & City Enterprise Boards and Area Partnerships.

Policy is determined by Forfás, which is the National Policy & Advisory Board for Enterprise, Trade, Science, Technology & Innovation, reporting to the Department of Enterprise, Trade & Employment.

IDA Ireland and Enterprise Ireland both report to Forfás and implement policy set by it. IDA Ireland focuses on inwards investment — bringing foreign multinationals into Ireland — while Enterprise Ireland is tasked with supporting indigenous (local) businesses.

There are also other State agencies whose role includes that of stimulating development, albeit often in specified sectors.

Where do I start?
Although there has been a huge shift away from a jobs focus among the enterprise support agencies, ironically the first question that you must answer to decide where you should look for help still relates to the employment potential of your new business.

If, within three years or so of start-up, you are likely still to employ under 10 people, you should make your way to the County & City Enterprise Boards and / or the other local support agencies.

Once you can show clearly that you are likely to employ more than 10 people within three years or so of start-up (and meet some other criteria, including demonstrating export potential), Enterprise Ireland (or Shannon Development / Údarás na Gaeltachta, as appropriate) classifies your business as a "high potential start-up" and takes you under its wing.

County & City Enterprise Boards

County & City Enterprise Boards (CEBs) are probably the most important source of assistance for the start-up business. The 35 CEBs around the country – one in each county, with additional CEBs in Cork and Dublin) aim to encourage local initiative. Each is a company limited by guarantee, and has an executive staff, headed by a Chief Executive Officer. The 12-14 Board members are drawn from elected members of the local authority, the social partners, State agencies, ICTU, IBEC, the farming organisations, the county manager and community and other representatives.

The CEBs have responsibility for enterprise development in areas not already covered by the State industrial development agencies – specifically, enterprises employing (or likely to employ) fewer than 10 persons and service businesses. Where they receive applications for funding and advice that are more appropriate to the remit of existing agencies (say, Enterprise Ireland), such applications are directed to the appropriate agency.

Each CEB has access to an Enterprise Fund which has been established to assist small projects. However, they do not normally consider proposals involving grant support in excess of €75,000 or projects with investment costs in excess of €150,000. Project promoters must demonstrate that:

o There is a market for the proposed product / service.

o Adequate overall finance will be available to fund the project.

o They possess the management and technical capacity to implement the proposed project.

o Projects to be assisted will add value so as to generate income or supplement income for those involved, and will have the capacity to create new direct employment whether full-time, part-time or seasonal, or will, as a minimum, contribute directly to maintaining employment in existing small businesses.

o They will comply with existing policies on tax clearance, the certification of subcontractors, and related matters.

The CEBs do not fund projects which are contrary to public policy, nor do they duplicate support for projects which would be eligible for assistance from any existing sectoral or grant structure, or which involve primary agricultural production.

The following core grants are available:

o A maximum of 50% of the cost of capital and other investment, or €75,000 – whichever is lower.

o An employment grant of €7,500 for each new person employed by the business.

o A maximum of 60% of the cost of preparing a feasibility study / business plan, subject to an overall limit of €6,350 (BMW regions; 50% to €5,100 in South & East) in the case of a single project.

Other specific grants – for web development, attendance at trade fairs, etc – also may be available but varies between CEBs and over time. Check locally for the current situation.

Assistance is not confined to grants, since the CEBs have authority to provide loans and loan guarantees and to take equity stakes in businesses. In addition, the CEBs act as a source of advice and information. Many provide training and mentoring services, which are both useful forms of support.

You should contact your local CEB before taking your project much beyond an initial stage. An initial informal discussion will quickly determine whether:

o The CEB can support your project.

o A feasibility study grant may be available.

o You should make changes to your project to make it acceptable to the CEB for assistance.

Enterprise Ireland

Enterprise Ireland is the government organisation charged with assisting the development of Irish enterprise. Its mission is: "to work in partnership with client companies to develop a sustainable competitive advantage, leading to a significant increase in profitable sales, exports and employment". Its clients are mainly manufacturing and internationally-traded services companies employing more than 10 people. Its services include:

o Access to business angels and venture capital funds.

o Assistance with feasibility studies.

o Assistance with intellectual property and technology transfer.

o Benchmarking.

o Design support.

o Incubation and workspaces.

o Linkages with EU technology support programmes.

o Market information and supports,

o Mentoring.

o Support for e-commerce / e-business.

Enterprise Ireland assists "high potential" start-ups:

o In manufacturing or internationally-traded services.

o Based on technological innovation or exploitable market niche opportunity.

o Likely to achieve projected sales of at least €1m and 10 jobs by Year 3.

o Export-oriented.

o Capable in the longer term of significantly exceeding these levels.

o Being established by experienced managers, academics or technical graduates.

Assistance provided by Enterprise Ireland nationally is provided in certain regions by Shannon Development or Údarás na Gaeltachta, as appropriate.

Enterprise Ireland's approach involves:

o Detailed analysis of a company's requirements.

o Determination of the level of need for State support.

o Targeting of funds to meet the real needs of the business.

o Provision of funds to companies that are forecast to deliver strong growth in both sales and exports.

There is a wide range of State, or State-supported, bodies that provide support of various kinds to would-be entrepreneurs. In addition, there are also many sources of private sector assistance – some on a pay-for basis and some free. For more information, see the appropriate categories in the Assistance section of **www.startingabusinessinireland.com** for a range of known sources; also see **Further Information**.

Working with financiers and State agencies

Entrepreneurs regularly make five mistakes in dealing with banks, investors and State agencies.

o They assume that they are entitled to funding or support.

o They don't understand the financier's or State agency's point-of-view.

- o They don't plan the timing of their approach.
- o They don't provide the information required for decision-making
- o They don't eliminate the risks for the financier / agency.

The reality is that you have NO entitlement to financing or support. Banks and investors are commercial organisations, which make decisions on whether to support your business based only on the benefit to them in doing so. State agencies have a duty to assist wherever and however they can within their remit but remain accountable to their sponsoring Department, and ultimately to the Department of Finance, for the use of public funds and so must be transparent in all their activities.

So, if you are to be successful in getting the support you need, you need to understand the other person's point-of-view. Back to three key questions in market research: Who are your customers? What are they really buying from you? Why do they buy from you? Apply these to your search for funding and support.

Bank managers are more concerned about getting back the money they have lent you (hence their interest in collateral and personal guarantees) than in how much profit you make or what your technology does. Investors are more interested in the upside for profit and will weigh this against the risk of failure. State agencies are required by law to focus on jobs, so your business's potential here weighs more with them than other factors. Understand this and you will stand out from the crowd.

While both financiers and State agencies try hard to be customer-focused, they have their own internal processes and procedures to adhere. Very rarely can the person you speak to make a final decision on their own – in most cases, especially where significant amounts of money are concerned, the decision must go to a committee. These committees meet at intervals – and, if one meeting is missed, decisions cannot be made until the next. So you need to plan your approach: find out when the next decision-making meeting takes place and what is the deadline for you to submit your proposal in order to reach that meeting. If that's not feasible, for whatever, reason, what's the next meeting date and deadline?

Also, in order to reach a decision, the committee usually requires certain information in a certain format. The person you are dealing with at the bank or agency will help insofar as they can with the formatting, but it's your responsibility to provide the basic information – they can't help you unless you provide it!

In addition, the bank manager or CEB officer is not an entrepreneur, they are not in the business of taking risk – that's your department! Identify the risks from their point-of-view, and do what you can to eliminate them. If you're planning to use a new technology, show where it's already working; if you're planning to sell product to a new market, show that this has already been done somewhere else. Make it safe for the bank / agency to make the decision you want.

Last, it's often useful to establish a relationship with the bank or agency in advance, if you can. Ask for a short meeting, explaining that you are still at the early thinking stage of starting a business and that you are looking for advice. Come with some good questions – and listen to the answers. The aim is not to get money or support from this meeting but to make the person / institution aware of you, so that when you return with a proposal they will be impressed with the progress you have made.

Remember, you may be dealing with a bank or a State agency – but, actually, you're dealing with one individual, person-to-person – make it count!

STARTING YOUR BUSINESS

The stages involved in a start-up include some that you have been through already – for example:

- o Assessing your own suitability and preparedness.
- o Finding an idea.
- o Evaluating your idea.
- o Looking for funding and assistance.

If you decide to proceed with your business idea and to start a business, you will need to

- o Decide on a legal structure.
- o Register for tax.
- o Register for any licences or permissions required.
- o Find premises.
- o Set up accounting systems.
- o Prepare financial projections.
- o Get the necessary finance.
- o Write a Business Plan.

More information on all of these stages is available in:

- o Starting Your Own Business: A Workbook, by Ron Immink & Brian O'Kane, published by Oak Tree Press (**www.oaktreepress.com**).
- o The website **www.startingabusinessinireland.com**.

o Start Your Own Business courses offered by the
County & City Enterprise Boards.

Any of these will take you through the process of starting a
business in more detail and guide you towards writing a
business plan, which is essential before you launch your
business.

Could You Be Your Own Boss? has given you enough
information to make an informed decision on whether
starting a business is the right opportunity for you going
forward. If it is, then go for it. If it's not, then you have
wasted very little time and effort and saved yourself
potentially a great deal of loss and heartache. Either way,
the best of luck to you!

FURTHER INFORMATION

Key sources of assistance for start-ups in Ireland include:

- AIB Bank – www.aib.ie
- Bank of Ireland – www.bankofireland.ie
- Bord Bia – www.bordbia.ie
- Business Incubation Centres
- Central Statistics Office – www.cso.ie
- County & City Enterprise Boards – www.enterpriseboards.ie
- Companies Registration Office – www.cro.ie
- Crafts Council of Ireland – www.ccoi.ie
- Enterprise Ireland – www.enterprise-ireland.com
- Failte Ireland – www.failteireland.ie
- FÁS – www.fas.ie
- First Step – www.first-step.ie
- Health & Safety Authority – www.hsa.ie
- Irish Franchise Association – www.irishfranchiseassociation.com
- LEADER+ companies – www.irishleadernetwork.org
- National Standards Authority of Ireland – www.nsai.ie
- Patents Office – www.patentsoffice.ie
- Revenue Commissioners – www.revenue.ie
- Shannon Development – www.shannondev.ie
- Údarás na Gaeltachta – www.udaras.ie
- Ulster Bank – www.ulsterbank.ie

For more information on these sources – and many more – see **www.startingabusinessinireland.com**.

And, you'll find more information and support at our website, **www.couldyoubeyourownboss.com**.

USEFUL TITLES FROM OAK TREE PRESS

Fire in the Belly: An Exploration of the Entrepreneurial Spirit
Yanky Fachler
€15 pb : ISBN 978-1-86076-210-9

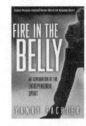

Before you start your own business, you have to successfully
navigate the mental transition from the world of employment – the
ladder world – to the entrepreneurial world. **Fire in the Belly** is
packed with case studies, quotations and anecdotes, much of it
based on the entrepreneurial workshops that the author conducts
in Ireland and abroad.

Grabbing the Oyster! Anecdotes & Advice from Icons of Irish Business
Pearce Flannery
€25 hb : ISBN-13: 978-1-904887-25-6

Read the stories of Denis Brosnan, Louis Copeland, Denis
Desmond, Declan Ganley, Liam Griffin, Anne Heraty, Michael
Herbert, Pat McDonagh, Padraig Ó Céidigh, Feargal Quinn, Niall
Quinn and James Sheehan and learn what makes them tick – and
how you can develop entrepreneurial traits yourself. These
entrepreneurs – and many more like them – are the people who
influence our employment figures, our GDP, our Government's
fiscal policy and, ultimately, the living standards of our citizens. From his
experiences with his own business, Pragmatica (**www.pragmatica.ie**), Pearce
Flannery has evaluated and extrapolated what he believes to be the common
denominators for success among all of these entrepreneurs.

STAR: Leadership Behaviours for Stellar SME Growth
Will McKee & John McKee
€35 hb : ISBN 978-1-904887-23-2

From consulting interventions with leaders and executive top
teams in SMEs, the authors have created a simple, real-life-based
model that clearly articulates leadership – in terms of vision, team-
building, selling, managing and innovation – around the goal of
stellar growth. It describes best-practice approaches using real-life
examples and demonstrates how to measure your own
competence across a range of critical behaviours.

USEFUL TITLES FROM OAK TREE PRESS

Starting a Business in Ireland (5th edition)
Brian O'Kane
€20 pb : ISBN 978-1-86076-267-3
The essential guide for anyone looking to go out on their own, **Starting a Business in Ireland** takes would-be entrepreneurs through all the stages in starting a business. New in this expanded edition is the most comprehensive directory ever assembled of State, EU and private sector organisations that provide assistance to start-ups and small businesses. Supported by the website, **www.startingabusinessinireland.com**. Over 30,000 copies sold!

Starting Your Own Business: A Workbook (2nd edition)
Ron Immink & Brian O'Kane
€20 pb : ISBN 978-1-86076-224-6
Commissioned originally in 1997 by the Department of Enterprise, Trade & Employment to meet a real need for practical, relevant information among would-be entrepreneurs, **Starting Your Own Business: A Workbook** has been updated / expanded to reflect changing trends in Irish small business. Supported by the website, **www.startingabusinessinireland.com**. Over 35,000 copies sold!

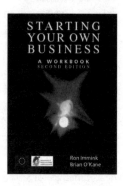

Oak Tree Press titles are available from all good bookshops and online from **www.oaktreepress.com**.